A Star's Purpose

Written and Illustrated by Abbigale McCarthy

Balboa Press books may be ordered through booksellers or by contacting:

Balboa Press
A Division of Hay House
1663 Liberty Drive
Bloomington, IN 47403
www.balboapress.com
1 (877) 407-4847

ISBN: 978-1-9822-3087-6 (sc)
ISBN: 978-1-9822-3088-3 (e)

Library of Congress Control Number: 2019909146

Print information available on the last page.

Balboa Press rev. date: 10/28/2019

BALBOA
PRESS
A DIVISION OF HAY HOUSE

To love.

One

There Once was a Star
She felt dim and alone.

Two

She was beautiful yet lonely,
deep space was her home.

Three

She saw in the distance an awesome planet...

Four

With colors green and blue
it was our home...

Five

The home of me and you!
The Star
was amazed...

Six

by the wonderful sphere.
She
gazed in wonder

Seven

and longed to be near.
Then one moment...

Eight

a feeling came.
I should move closer...
No... I should remain...

Nine

She wanted to shine for the planet much like the sun.

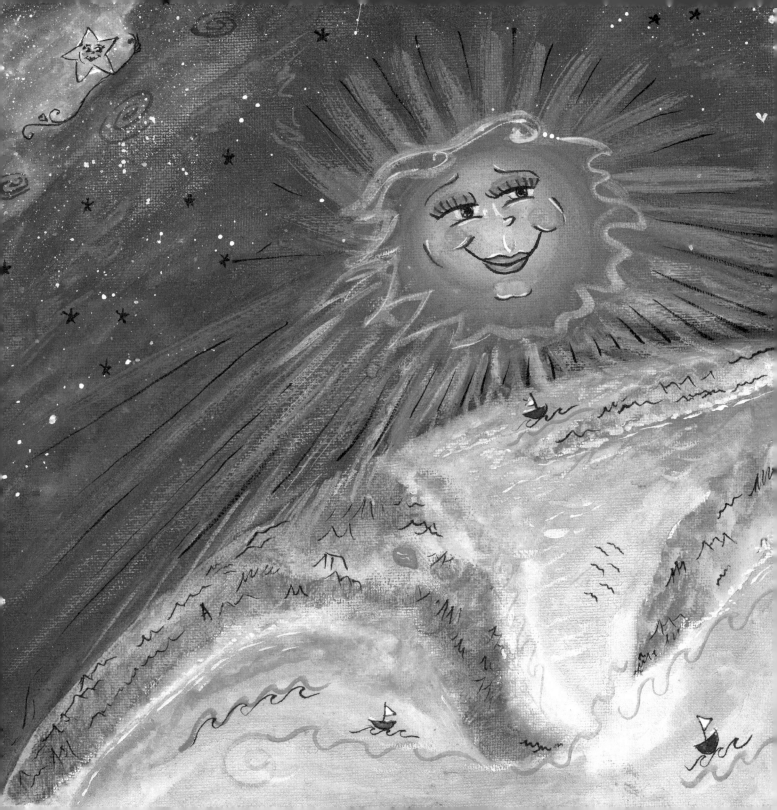

Ten

She wanted people to see her. She wanted some fun.

Eleven

She made the decision, she moved closer in.

Twelve

Then from the ground...
some Kings would begin.

So it begins...

Abbigale McCarthy is an Author, Illustrator and Teacher.
She lives in Southern California with her Husband and their two Children.

Printed in the United States
By Bookmasters